Atair, Kat, Bawah
or
Top, Near, Bottom

Buku 4

Book 4 - Prepositions

Chakapan Baba Ni Ari series

Baba Malay Today series

All Rights Reserved.
No part of this publication may be reproduced, stored in a retrieval system, or transmitted, in any form or by any means electronic, mechanical, photocopying, recording or otherwise, without the prior written permission of the publishers.

Theresa Fuller asserts the moral right to be identified as the author of this work.

Bare Bear Media

ISBN 978-1-925748-20-8 - Print
ISBN 978-1-026748-21-5 - Ebook

Cover by Helzkat Designs

Copyright January 2023©

Sincere thanks to my husband, Paul, who supported this work in every way possible. I love you.

National Library of Australia
US Library of Congress - TXu 2-356-888

Published 16th of June 2023

Introduction - Prepositions

Language is powerful.

In writing this text, I applied the SHOW don't TELL method. I wanted the reader to be able to pick up this book and begin to learn. Much as you would pick up a game and play.

>Chobak.

>To try.

The next four rules I wish to expound are these:

>1. Subject + Verb + Object + Preposition + Subject/Object.

>2. Subject + Verb + Object + Informal Preposition + Preposition + Subject/Object

>3. Subject + Verb + Object + Formal Preposition + Preposition + Subject/Object

>4. Informal/Formal Preposition + Preposition + Subject/Object

At the end of the day, have fun.

This is Baba Malay, the language of the Peranakans.

>**YOUR** language.

Baba Malay

Baba Malay is the language of my ancestors.

A language that I discovered late in 2021 was about to go extinct with fewer than a thousand speakers in the world. I took a course in Baba Malay taught by Kenneth Chan, author of *BABA MALAY FOR EVERYONE - A comprehensive guide to the Peranakan language*. This was my start to saving Baba Malay.

But I believed much more had to be done.

The book you hold in your hands is the result of my mad persistence to save my language. While there are books out there on Baba Malay, I found little in the way for children. As a teacher, I believe that to save a language we must start with the young.

I wanted a book that parents could give to their children.
One I could give to my kids.

This is my attempt.

Theresa, affectionately known in the Peranakan community as Bibek Theresa.

Sydney,
29th of May, 2022

Chobak

Chobak = To Try

I love Baba Malay.

Contents

Introduction	3
Baba Malay	4
Kat - At, In, On, Near, Over	8
Di - At, In	9
Atair/Atas - Top, Above	10
Bawah - Below, Beneath, Bottom, Under	11
Chobak - Kat/Di/Atair/Bawah	12
Depan - In Front	14
Belakang - Behind	15
Lagik - From	16
Sampay - Until, To arrive, To reach	17
Dalam - In, Inside	18
Sebelah - Beside, On one side, Next To, Over	19
Dari - From	20
Buat - For	21
Sama - With	22
Pasair/Pasal - About	23
Seberang - Across	24
Masok - Including	25
Forms of Prepositions in English	26
Notes	30
About the Author	31
More books in the Baba Malay Today Series	32

KAT - At, In, On, Near, Over

Basket = Bakol

'KAT' is a general preposition. Prepositions show direction, time, place, location, spatial relationships or introduce an object. 'KAT' is derived from the word 'Dekat' meaning **'Near'**.

Pikol ayer kat bakol. (Idiom: meaning to do the impossible)
Carry water in a basket.

Saya tinggair kat 7 Wallaby Way.
I live at 7 Wallaby Way.

Lu tinggair kat mana kat Sydney?
You live at where in Sydney?

Tarok mangkok kat (atair) piring.
Put the bowl on (top) of the plate.

Note: When 'KAT' is used as 'ON', using either 'ATAIR/ATAS' i.e., top or 'BAWAH' i.e., 'bottom', helps avoid any ambiguity regarding location. (See pages 10 & 11.)

Kat sana ada sekolah.
Near that place is a school.

Kat sini.
Over here.

DI - At, In

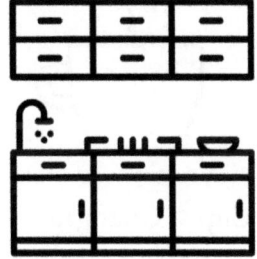

Kitchen = Dapor

While **'KAT'** is the informal manner, **'DI'** or **'DI-'** is formal.

Di bawah rumah ni ada dapor.
At the bottom of this house is the kitchen.

Gua tinggair di Sydney.
I live in Sydney.

Mary di-mana? Dia tak di-sini.
Where is Mary? She is not here.

Glossary
Ada = Have/Has
Ayer = Water
Bakol = Basket
Dapor = Kitchen
Kueh = Cake
Mangkok = Bowl
Pikol = Carry
Piring = Plate
Sana = There
Sekolah = School
Tarok = Put
Tinggair = Live

ATAIR/ATAS - Top, Above

Cup = Changkir

'ATAIR' and **'ATAS'** can be used by themselves or with **'KAT'** or **'DI'**.

Gua tarok changkir atair piring.
I put the cup top of the plate.

Again, we use 'Kat' as an informal preposition to express direction or place. 'Di' is more formal.

Gua tarok changkir kat atair piring.
I put the cup on top of the plate.

Bintang kat atair kita.
The stars are above us.

Tarok piring di atair mangkok.
Put the plate on top of the bowl.

Kita pi loteng. Kita pi atair loteng. Kita pi loteng atair.
We go upstairs. We go upstairs. We go to the uppermost floor.

Glossary
Bintang = Stars
Changkir = Cup
Kita = We/Us
Loteng = Upstairs or Upper Floor
Mangkok = Bowl
Piring = Plate

Gua mesti belajair Chakapan Baba.

BAWAH - Below, Beneath, Bottom, Under

Bowl = Mangkok

'**BAWAH**' can be used by itself or with '**KAT**' or '**DI**'.

Saya tarok mangkok besair bawah mangkok kechik.
I put the big bowl under the little bowl.

(Note: In Baba Malay adjectives generally come after nouns.)

Saya tarok mangkok kat bawah piso.
I put the bowl under the knife.

Saya mo tarok garfu di bawah mangkok.
I want to put the fork under the bowl.

Saya pi loteng bawah. Saya pi bawah loteng.
I go downstairs.

Saya pi **loteng bawah**. (Note: Other meaning for **loteng bawah**.)
I go to the bottom most floor.

Glossary
Atair Loteng = Upstairs
Besair = Big
Garfu = Fork
Kechik = Small
Loteng Atair = Uppermost Floor
Loteng Bawah = Downstairs or Bottom most Floor
Mo = Want
Piso = Knife   Tarok = Put/Place

CHOBAK - KAT/DI/ATAIR/BAWAH

Upstairs = Loteng

Select the correct word

I put the cake on top of the table.
e.g. Gua tarok kueh (kat/di/(atair)/bawah) meja.

1. I live in Singapore.
   Saya tinggair (kat/atair/bawah) Singapore/Singapura.

2. I went over there.
   Saya pi (kat/di/atair/bawah) sana.

3. I go upstairs. (Informal)
   Gua pi (di atair/kat atair) loteng.

4. I live near there.
   Saya tinggair (kat/kat bawah/di/di bawah) sana.

5. Put the bowl in the kitchen. (Formal)
   Tarok mangkok (kat/di/atair/bawah) dalam dapor.

Answers: 1. Kat. 2. Kat. 3. Kat Atair. 4. Kat. 5. Di.

CHOBAK - KAT/DI/ATAIR/BAWAH

Plate = Piring

Select the correct word

1. Dia tarok piring kat bawah mangkok.
   He put the plate (at/in/on/under/near) the bowl.

2. Dia pi loteng atair.
   She went (uppermost floor/upstairs/up up and away).

3. Bawah loteng ada dapor.
   (Above, Below, In, At) the upper floor is a kitchen.

4. Saya tinggair kat 123 Cockatoo Crescent.
   I live (at/in/above/beneath) 123 Cockatoo Cresecent.

5. Saya kat bawah loteng.
   I am (at, in, on, near over) the bottom floor.

Answers: 1.Under. 2. Uppermost Floor or Upstairs. 3. Below. 4. At. 5. At or On.

DEPAN - In front

School = Sekolah

'DEPAN' means **'In front of.'** Most likely from the word 'Hadapan'. 'Kat' and 'Di' may precede it.

1. Ada satu pokok depan 7 Wallaby Way.
   There is a tree in front of 7 Wallaby Way.

2. Piring kechik depan piring besair.
   The small plate is in front of the big plate.

3. Depan dia mia mata ada dua burung.
   Before her eyes were two birds.

4. Saya pi sekolah minggu depan.
   I will go to school next week.

5. Buka pintu depan. (Note: Pintu Depan = Main Door (Or Pintu Besair))
   Open the front door.

6. Pusing depan.
   Turn to the front.

7. Tentang depan mata tak nampak. (Saying)
   Unable to see or not aware.

BELAKANG - Behind

Singapore

Just as 'DEPAN' denotes 'Front', **'BELAKANG'** denotes **'Behind.'**

1. Ada satu pokok belakang 7 Wallaby Way.
   There is a tree behind 7 Wallaby Way.

2. Piring kechik kat belakang piring besair.
   The small plate is behind the big plate.

3. Dia orang depan lain belakang lain. (Idiom)
   He is doubled-faced.

4. Pusing di belakang.
   Turn to the back.

5. Besok belakang ari, saya pi Singapore.
   In time to come (or the future), I will go to Singapore.

Glossary
Depan mata = In full view/before the eyes (Mata = Eye/s)
Burung = Bird/s
Kereta = Car
Kerja = Work
Lain = Other, Different
Minggu Depan = Next week or the following week
Nampak = See, Tak Nampak = Not See
Pokok = Tree or plant
Tengok = See

LAGIK - From

Shirley

'**LAGIK**' means '**From**.' Another form of 'From' is 'DARI', see page 20.

Saya datang lagik Australia.
I come from Australia.

Daisy lagik Sydney.
Daisy is from Sydney.

Shirley lagik Singapore.
Shirley is from Singapore.

Glossary
Datang = Come

Other forms of usage for Lagik
Apa Lagik = what's more. Besides. Moreover.
Belom Lagik = Not as yet
Bikin Lagik = Made from
Lagik, Laik, Lagi = More. Still. Yet more
Lagik Tadik = Since just now
Lagik Sikit or Sikit Lagik = Nearly. Almost. A little more.
Lagik Baik = It is best
Lagikan = Since, Ever, Since
Lebeh Lagik = Even much more
Sikit Ari Lagik = In a few day's time. Before long
Tinggair Lagik = Except

SAMPAY - Until, To arrive, To reach

Driving = Bawak Kereta

'**SAMPAY**' means 'To Attain', 'To reach (a destination)', 'Until', 'To Arrive.'

Dia bawak kereta sampay Johore Bahru.
He drove until Johore Bahru.

Boon Keng makan sampay kenyang.
Boon Keng ate until he was full.

Beng Loon sampay kat Singapore Ari Ampat.
Beng Loon arrived at Singapore on Thursday.

Geok Eng naik tangga sampay loteng atair.
Geok Eng climbed up the stairs until she reached the top floor.

Glossary
Bawak Kereta = Drove
Kenyang = Full
Makan = Ate or Eat
Naik Tangga = Climbed up the stairs

Other forms of usage for Sampay
Mana Sampay = Everywhere. Wherever. At every opportunity.
Sampay Ati = Have you the heart (to do this)

All of you must learn Baba Malay.

DALAM - In, Inside

Prawn = Udang

'DALAM' means '**Inside**.' 'Kat' and 'Di' may precede it.

Dalam dapor ni ada manyak laok embok-embok.
In this kitchen there is a lot of Peranakan food.

Tarok duit di-dalam bag ni.
Put the money in this bag.

Dia macham kodok dalam skol.
He is like a frog in a well. (Idiom: An untravelled person with a limited perspective.)

Dia mia liu macham udang dalam tenggok.
His big brother is trapped. (Udang dalam tenggok = Prawn in a trap.)

NOTE: There is no direct translation for some aspects of Baba Malay such as 'out' as a preposition.

Amekkan tu kueh lagik bakòl. Keluairkan tu kueh lagik bakol.
Take that cake from the basket. Out that cake from the basket.

Glossary
Duit = Money
Luair = Outer, external, exterior
Di-luair = Outside. (From Luair/luar meaning outer/external/exterior)
Keluair = To go out
Keluairkan = To bring or take out

Chakapan Baba lagik baik.

SEBELAH - Beside, On one Side, Next To, Over

Fork and spoon = Sendok-Garfu

'**SEBELAH**' derived from 'BELAH' meaning '**Split**', '**Cleft**' or '**Slit.**' 'Kat' and 'Di' may precede it.

Garfu sebelah sendok.
The fork is beside the spoon. The fork is on one side of the spoon. The fork is next to the spoon.

Mari kita pi sebelah sini.
Let us go over here.

Glossary
Kodok = Frog
Laok Embok-embok = Peranakan Food
Macham = Like
Manyak = Plenty
Skol = Well
Udang = Prawn/s

Other forms of usage for Sebelah
Sebelah Sini = Over here. On this side
Sebelah Sana = Over there. On that side
Sebelah Membelah = Right next to one another. Neighbours
Sebelah Mata Takleh Liat = Intolerable
Sebelah = One of a pair
Berat Sebelah = Heavy on one side. Showing favouritism
Buang Sebelah = Aside from. Besides
Dengair Kuping Sebelah = A tendency to listen to one side of the story

DARI - From

Pot = Periok

Like 'Lagik' on Page 16, **'DARI'** means **'From.'**

Dia datang dari situ.
He came from there.

Dari puncha, dia selalu baik.
From the beginning, she was always good.

Kita datang dari jauh.
We came from afar.

Dari mulai, dia tak suka belajair.
From the beginning, she never liked studying.

Apasair lorang tak ambek periok dari dapor?
Why did all of you not take the pot from the kitchen?

Glossary

Badan Kuat = Exercise
Belajair = Study
Bikin = To make, To do, or To produce
Gulong = Roll
Jauh = Far
Lorang = You (the plural form)
Mulai = Begin
Puncha = Beginning, Source

BUAT - For

Swimming = Berenang

As a preposition, '**BUAT**' means '**For**' and functions to show purpose.

Michael berenang buat badan kuat.
Michael swims for exercise.
(In the above eg., the intended purpose for swimming is exercise.)

Lu bikin kueh, buat apa?
You make cakes, for what? Or What did you make cakes for?
(What is its intended purpose?)

Tua Ee gulong popiah buat saya mia ari besair.
Tua Ee rolls popiah for my birthday.
(The intended purpose is for a birthday- ari besair.)

Other forms of usage for BUAT
Apa Boleh buat = What can one do? It can't be helped.
Buat Turun = Take down
Buat Tang = To bring
Buat Pi = To carry away elsewhere
Buat Naik = To carry up
Buat Masok = To bring in
Buat Keluair = To take out
Buatkan = Cause
Buat Pa = Whatever for

SAMA - With

Hockey = Hockey

'**SAMA**' means '**same**', '**identical**'.

As a preposition, '**SAMA**' means '**Along with**' or '**Together.**'

'Sama' is used to say that people or things are in a place together or else doing an activity with each other.

    Sentence 1:   Alison tinggair kat 12 Orchard Road.
                            Alison lives at 12 Orchard Road.

    Sentence 2:   Anne tinggair kat 12 Orchard Road.
                            Anne lives at 12 Orchard Road.

    Joined: Alison **SAMA** Anne tinggair kat 12 Orchard Road.
            Alison **SAME WITH** Anne live at 12 Orchard Road.
            Alison **TOGETHER WITH** Anne live at 12 Orchard Road.

    (Sama tends to function more as the conjunction 'AND'.)
    Alison **AND** Anne live at 12 Orchard Road.

The word '**SAMA**' is also the closest thing that Baba Malay has to the conjunction '**AND**'.

Chakapan Baba lu punya chakapan.

PASAIR/PASAL - About

Big sister with little sister = Tachi sama adek prompuan

As a preposition, '**PASAIR**' or '**PASAL**' means '**About**.'
As a conjunction, 'PASAIR' or 'PASAL' means 'Because.'
As a noun, 'PASAIR' or 'PASAL' means 'Market'. Always look at the context.

'**PASAIR**' is used to say that something is on the subject or else connected with.

Tu buku pasair cherita Baba.
That book is about Peranakan stories.

Kita chakap pantat pasair Sophie.
We were gossiping about Sophie.

When 'PASAIR' is linked with 'tu' it means 'so' or 'so because of that.'

Example: Gua mia adek prompuan mo duit, **PASAIR TU** dia kerja.
My younger sister wants money, **SO BECAUSE OF THAT** she works.

Glossary
Adek Jantan = Younger brother
Adek Prompuan = Younger Sister
Chakap Pantat = Gossip
Masak = Cook
Tachi = Big Sister

Baba Malay is your language.

SEBERANG - Across

Bridge = Jambatan

'**SEBERANG**' means 'To **cross over to the other side**' or '**Opposite side or Opposite bank**'.

As a preposition, 'SEBERANG' is used to show movement from one side to the other side of something clearly delimited. Examples of things that have clear limits are areas of land, a building, a street or even a waterway.

Susie Maroney berenang seberang English Channel.
Susie Maroney swam across the English Channel.

Saya mia sekolah seberang ni jalan.
My school is on the opposite side of the road.

Kita lari seberang jambatan.
We ran across the bridge.

Gua mia bapak bawak kereta seberang Singapore.
My father drove across Singapore.

Glossary
Belajair = Learn/Study
Berenang = Swim
Jambatan = Bridge
Lari = Run

MASOK - Including

Rice = Nasi or Nasik

'**MASOK**' means 'To enter' or 'To become'.

As a preposition, 'MASOK' is used to show that a person or object is part of a particular group, event or amount.

Saya mia anak-beranak masok saya mia anjing, suka makan nasi.
My family including my dog, loves eating rice.

Saya ada sa-ratus dollar masok saya mia duit dalam saya mia piggy bank.
I have one hundred dollars including my money in my piggy bank.

Glossary
Anak-Beranak = Family
Anjing = Dog
Sa-ratus = 100
Dollar = Dollar or Ringgit. (This is the contemporary context for currency. Duit means money.)

Other forms of usage for Masok
Buat Masok = To bring in
Masok Angin = Affected by the wind element
Masok Mata = Agreeable to the eye
Masok Perangkap = To fall into a trap

Forms of Prepositions in English

About	- Pasair, Pasal
Above	- Atair
Across	- Seberang
Across the other side	- Seberang
After	- Lepair(alus), lepas(kasar). See page 27 opposite.
Against	- Technically, no exact term. See page 27 opposite.
Among	- Technically, no exact term. See page 28.
At	- Dekat, Di, Kat
Behind	- Belakang
Beside	- Sebelah
Below	- Bawah
Bottom	- Bawah
Down	- Bawah
During	- Technically, no exact term. See page 28.
For	- Buat
From	- Dari, Lagik, Sampay
Front	- Depan
In	- Dalam, Dekat, Di, Kat
Including	- Masok
In front	- Depan
Inside	- Dalam, Dekat, Kat
Into	- Dalam, Dekat, Kat
Near	- Dekat, Kat
Next to	- Sebelah
Of	- Technically, no exact term. See page 28.
On	- Dekat, Kat
On one side	- Sebelah
Out	- Technically there is no exact term for this. See page 18.
Over	- Atair, Dekat, Kat
Since	- Lagik, Lagik Tadik
To	- Kat
Top	- Atair(alus), Atas(kasar)
Under	- Bawah

Until - Sampay
With - Sama

Lepair

Saya mo pi jalan **lepair** makan.
I want to go for a walk after food.

Lepair itu, kita boleh main kebun.
After that, we can garden.

Sekarang **lepair** jam saya pi kerja.
Now it is past the time I go to work.

Other forms of usage for **Lepair**
Lepairkan napsu = To give vent to one's desire
Lepair = can also mean to let loose
Lepair garam = To let loose pent up anger
Lepair chakap = To pass the word around
Lepair ari = To see through the day.

Against

Ben berenang lawan (to fight **against**) gelombang.
Ben swam **against** the waves.

Dia lawan dia mia musoh.
He fought **against** his enemies.

Saya chondongkan diri sebelah tembok.
I leant **against** the wall.

Among

Kita tinggair sama orang asli.
We live **among** the natives.

Ada satu kuching sama burung komba.
There is a cat **among** the pigeons.

Kongsikan ni barang sama lorang.
Share this **among** yourselves.

During

Bila tempu Covid, seluru dunia tak senang.
During Covid, the world suffered.

Saya suka main bila tempu saya tak kreja.
I like to play **during** my break.

Of

Pasair tikus sama manusia.
(Because) **Of** mice and men.

Dia kawan saya.
He is a friend **of** mine.

Satu kilogram epel.
A kilogram **of** apples.

Atair dia mia kepala.
The top **of** his head.

Glossary

Barang = Things
Berenang = Swim
Bila = When
Bila Tempu = During
Burung Komba = Pigeons
Chondang = Slanting. Leaning. Incline to one side.
Dari dulu sampay sekarang = From the past until now
Dia = He/She/It
Dia Mia = His/Hers/Its
Diri = Oneself, Self, To stand
Dunia = World
Epel = Apple/s
Gelombang = Waves
Harta Dunia = Things of the world
Kawan = Friend
Kepala = Head
Kerja or Kreja = Work   Tak Kreja = Break/Unemployed
Kongsikan = Share
Kuching = Cat
Lawan = To fight against. To oppose.
Lorang = All of you or Yourselves
Main = Play
Manusia = Humans
Orang Asli = Natives
Satu = One
Sekarang = Later, Nowadays, Now
Seluru = Whole, Throughout all over
Seluru Dunia = All over the world
Shorga Dunia = Heaven on earth or Earthly paradise
Tembok = Wall
Tempu = Time
Tempu Dulu = Of old, In olden times
Tikus = Mice

NOTES

Baba Malay or Chakapan Baba or the Baba language was born when Chinese traders sailed down to Southeast Asia and intermarried with the local women. A mix of Hokkien and Malay, Baba Malay went into decline after WWII as many Peranakans were killed.

This is the reason why there are no Baba Malay equivalent to some words today. When in doubt English words are often used.

There are also two variants to Baba Malay:

1. Alus i.e., a refined form that women tended to speak
2. Kasair i.e., a coarser version practised by men.

Baba Malay tended to be spoken rather than written so there are many variations in the spelling e.g.,

kreja or kerja (work)

When in doubt I referred to Kenneth Chan's *Baba Malay For Everyone - A comprehensive guide to the Peranakan language* as well as William Gwee Thian Hock's *A Baba Malay Dictionary*.

Baba Malay is also sadly considered an endangered language.

Let's do our best to change this!

Bibek Theresa

About the Author

Theresa Fuller

Theresa Fuller has always loved stories and story-telling, but it was not until the birth of her first son that she became a full-time writer. Her aim was to write stories about her culture: Southeast Asia.

Theresa was Head of Computing at various private schools in Sydney. She has also been a Higher School Certificate (HSC) Examiner and HSC Assessor. Her teaching degrees have seen her work in primary and secondary schools and at Kalgoorlie College in Western Australia.

Her first published novel in 2018 was *THE GHOST ENGINE*, a steampunk fantasy about the fictitious granddaughter of Ada Lovelace, the world's first programmer. Theresa has published two books on Southeast Asian mythology: *THE GIRL WHO BECAME A GODDESS* (2019) and *THE GIRL SUDAN PAINTED LIKE A GOLD RING* (2022).

In 2020, Theresa lost many family members. She threw heself into researching her family history as a way to deal with her grief. This was when she discovered that the language of her ancestors - Baba Malay - was on the verge of extinction. As a writer, teacher and selfpublishing author, Theresa found herself in an unusual position - she was able to create the curriculum that was needed to help fill a vacuum.

The result is the **Baba Malay Today** series.

All in aid of saving the language.

www.theresafuller.com

Thank you for your support!

More Books in the Baba Malay Today Series

Book 1 - Interrogatory Part I   SAPA, APA, MANA *or*
WHO, WHAT, WHERE

Book 2 - Interrogatory Part II   AMCHAM, APASAIR, BILA *or*
HOW, WHY, WHEN

Book 3 - Conjunctions   TAPI, ABIS, PASAIR *or*
BUT, SO, BECAUSE

Book 4 - Prepositions   ATAIR, KAT, BAWAH *or*
TOP, NEAR, BOTTOM

Book 5 - Antonyms   ALUS, KA, KASAR *or*
DELICATE, OR, COARSE

Book 6 - Essence   CHAKAPAN BABA ATI *or*
THE HEART OF BABA MALAY

Dear Reader,

Thank you for the purchase of this book.

Please help us spread the word as we try to save our language.

Bibek Theresa

Sydney, 18th of June, 2022

Ingram Content Group UK Ltd.
Milton Keynes UK
UKHW020721260623
424053UK00014B/666